Conversations
with a
Sardonic Therapist

Anh Thien Ta, LMFT
(Ta-Kieu Thien Anh)
with
contributions by
Mafalda Neto Soares

Fuck Your Rules, You Need Change

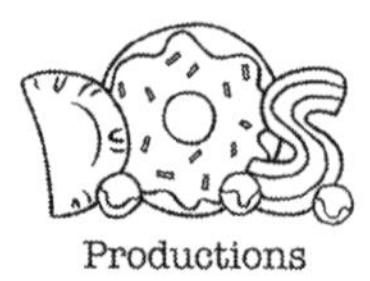

Donuts on Sunday Productions, LLC
(www.donutsonsundayproductions.com)
Livermore, CA

ISBN: 978-1-964260-10-5

For inquiries about special use or bulk purchases contact Donuts On Sunday Productions, LLC (DonutsOnSundayProductions@gmail.com).

Dedication

This acknowledgement is for those whose lives I have learned lessons with and from - the very truths which form the basis of the books that formed my formal academic education. Your lives taught and gave reference for others to get academic degrees. You are the primary source of resilience and wisdom. This book just reminds you of what You have Taught Me.

This book is dedicated:

- To those who have shared space, time, and energy with me.
- To my family, whose lessons we often learned the hard way.
- To those who visit our lives and leave so soon, may they discover and experience what we treasure in the lost and found.
- And to those whose path brought you here, whose way is being explored and discovered -

Welcome Home…
Where the lost can be found.

Format

Because it was recommended by someone I trust, I will add information on what to expect from this book.

This book, though it may be helpful, is NOT a self-help book.

This book is a combination of insights, stories and experiences for you, the reader, to relate to. The book sections will contain my own notes, stories, lessons, guiding principles, and reflections, usually in that order.

Preface:

Whether or not you can relate to the contents of the book, that's a you problem, not a me problem.

And even if you don't learn any lessons from the contents, somebody you know may benefit from it - simply give the book to them so they can either think you are an asshole or be graciously appreciative to you for potentially changing their lives.

If these conversations sound like you, don't be ridiculous, any likeness to persons, people, or ideas, fictional or not, is merely coincidental.

These stories are inspired by actual conversations with no particular person in mind, just universal experiences across time.

“Remember everyone, 'Listen' shares the same letters as the word 'Silent'.

In our magic bond, we must be silent in our minds, bodies, and spirits to listen to and become aware of the truth and magic of what is said and unsaid, seen and unseen.

'License' and 'Silence' also share the same magic letters. To have internal silence is to give license for the external to be seen, heard, known, and understood.”

Becoming aware…

Therapist's Note:
Why You are Here

If You are Here,
You are Either
an Asshole to other People,
People are Assholes to You,
or Maybe it is Both
or Perhaps,
You're an Asshole to Yourself

Storytime:
If people are assholes to you...
(Do you really have to ask yourself why?)

Therapist: Let's get this straight. You are here because sometimes other people make you feel like you are not good enough, or like you are unlovable, or that you are the source of their pain.

Client: ...yeah...

Therapist: Well as much as they are assholes to you, the first and biggest bully and asshole is you- for believing and agreeing with them. You are the leader of assholes, the champion and the best of the best at beating yourself up.

You chose their warped opinions over yourself. Stop being mean to yourself. Stop bullying yourself, and stop gaslighting yourself; maybe then, you might stop being the leader and trendsetter for the asshole mob that bullies you.

Quit being the first asshole to yourself.

Storytime:
Wait, so I'm the asshole?

(Scenario 1: People are the problem, not me!)

Therapist: Being an asshole is a choice- so just choose not to be an asshole.

Client: I can't help it. People are ________ (insert judgment or adjective here) and I have (insert reaction here, i.e. anger) issues.

Therapist: No, you have issues and (insert negative reactions such as anger here) is how you express them.

Client: I can't control it; I get (insert feeling here, i.e. mad) and just lose it.

Therapist: Thank you for naming that you are an uncontrollable asshole. Name it to tame it. You want control? Do you want to stop being an asshole?

Client: Well yeah. I also want people to stop being _______ (insert judgment or adjective here)...

Therapist: Then first stop being an asshole to them and foremost, yourself.

Client: …

Therapist: In summary- it starts with yourself. Hurt people will hurt people. You are hurting, you just won't admit it. You are limping but acting like it's a confident and intentional walk, and then you get upset at everyone else for walking away from your pretentious "anger". Let's be honest with ourselves. If we lie, we will never know what we are working with and what is truly in the way of being our best selves- regardless of what people say or do to us.

Anger and annoyance is depression and frustration facing outwards.

The real struggle is within.

Storytime:
Wait, so I'm the asshole?
(Scenario 2: I'm an asshole to people...)

I am the problem. It's my fault, I'm not (insert positive trait here) [enough]!

Therapist: You are your own WORST enemy; You are the leader of assholes to yourself. The leader of bullying who you are.

If you can beat your worst enemy, that makes you the champion and the best. So be the best at loving yourself.

Being an asshole is a choice - so just choose not to be an asshole to others, but first start with yourself.

Client: I can't help it. I am ________ (insert judgment or adjective here) and I have (insert reaction here, i.e. anger) issues.

Therapist: No, you have issues and (insert negative reactions such as anger here) is how you express them. ***Yes this is basically the same response - because the issue is really still the same isn't it?***

Client: I can't control it; I get (insert feeling here, i.e. mad) and feel things won't get better.

Therapist: Thank you for naming that you are an uncontrollable asshole that sees no hope to the end of your self bullying. Name it to tame it. You want control? Do you want to stop being an asshole to yourself?

Client: Well yeah. I don't think I am _______ (insert judgment or adjective here) enough...

Therapist: Like I said, then first stop being an asshole to yourself.

Client: …

Therapist: In summary. Hurt people will hurt people. You are hurting. So you hurt others trying to fill a hole inside. You are so focused on this feeling of a giant hole in you, that you feel you may be broken or there is something you are missing as a person. You are so focused on a deficit that you can't see the garden around the hole and have forgotten how to dream and envision what flowers could be planted in the hole.

Depression is just anger facing inwards.

Therapist's Lesson:
Three domains of Awareness
AND Knowledge:

1) The things you are Aware of and Know Something about it

2) The things you are Aware of and Know Nothing about it

3) The things you are Not even Aware exist, and therefore Know Nothing about it.

Guiding principle #1:

If You want to Tame it, you must Name it.

Therapist Reflection:

(If that principle didn't make sense to you, a self-help book would definitely not be for you. You need more than your own help. Luckily, this is not a self-help book. I hope you find it helpful nonetheless).

Becoming aware that something needs to change is always the first step towards change.

You cannot change something you cannot identify.
Be honest, so what kind of Asshole are You AND how have you contributed to the situation?

“Hope is just remaining open to the idea that things can change. There will always be a chance things will be in your favor or against it. We just often hope that things go in our favor.”

Considering Change…

Therapist's Note:
Narrative Medicine

If you made it this far, let's begin…

Narrative medicine is ancient strong medicine and storytelling is our tool. You are here to get your tools sharpened and medicine refined because yours are broken ass pieces of caustic shit.

We can only change what we are aware of and hope to be different; otherwise we are just aware and stuck in misery.

You are here because you know something is off and you want something different. Let us envision how life can be… away from the poisonous trash we choose to hang on to.

Storytime:
Insight

Client: I am only here because my (insert person you claim you care about) made me.

Therapist: So you don't think you have anything to work on. Do you feel coerced?

Client: Well, yeah. I am just fine and handling things on my own. I don't need therapy.

Therapist: Well you did request the appointment. How is "handling things" working out for you?

Client: I am only doing this because they are making me. So what do we do? You going to therapize me already?

Therapist: Nope. First session is always to see if there is a presenting problem. But since you can't name a problem except that you are being forced to do something, perhaps you need to assess how to work on the relationship you're in or consider leaving it. Who wants to be in a relationship that forces them to do anything anyway?

Client: That's crazy. Why would I leave the relationship? I am doing this to stay in it. If I don't do this, they said they'd leave me.

Therapist: So you are in a coercive relationship. That sounds like abuse to me.

Client: Don't put words in my mouth.

Therapist: I apologize if I misunderstood you. You said you were forced to do this. Do you find you have difficulty communicating with your partner or others?

Client:... Can we just get this over with? Or is there someone else I can talk to?

Therapist: Yes and Yes. Let me know and we can end this conversation and you can find another therapist to schedule with. And just to be very clear, you are the one being forced to seek a therapist, not me. So why did they "force" you into therapy?

Client: I'm already here. Let's just get this over with.

I am here because we argue a lot. Over small things. I think we are just stressed because we only argue when we are stressed.

Therapist: So what are some of the stressors?

Client: Finances, work stress, having so much on my mind that I become forgetful or easily distracted sometimes.

Therapist: Do you feel less energized lately?

Client: Not really.

Therapist: Does it take you awhile to fall asleep because you can't stop your thoughts or worries?

Client: Well, yeah. Everybody has that problem.

Therapist: Really? Have you asked everyone? Are you assuming? Let's mutually agree to not put words in each other's mouths, because I don't have that problem of falling asleep.

Client: So that's just one problem.

Therapist: So what are the other ones?

Client: .....

Therapist: I am glad you are able to list at least one problem now and how it clearly impacts your sleep and possibly that exhaustion impacts your relationship. Do you know how you contribute to the arguments?

Client: Yes. I get impatient and then we argue.

Therapist: I would add, you get defensive and then miscommunication happens.

Client: Well yeah, because I am right.

Therapist: Like how you don't need therapy but have difficulty communicating yourself in a way that people can understand you...

Client:...

Therapist: Feel free to fire me. Finding a therapist is like finding transportation or a car. Test drive them and try it out and commit when you find one that meets your needs in style, comfort, and efficacy.

We can continue if you'd like a full assessment, or just fire me now.

Client: ... yeah... let's finish this at least...

Therapist's Lesson:
Three levels of Insight

Level 1: Knowing there is a problem

Level 2: Knowing there is a problem and how it impacts you

Level 3: Knowing there is a problem and how you contribute to it.

(If you don't think you have any problems,
You actually may be other People's Problem)

Guiding Principle # 2:

In any given situation or circumstance, you will have to:

1) Accept what is and Embrace it or Wallow about it

2) Change what is

3) Change your Expectation of it.

Be clear, whatever it is you do, it is a choice you ultimately make; nobody else can choose for you.

Therapist's Reflection:

We are all like plants, we never stop growing.

We do not grow backwards; we always grow forward.

We will grow forward in the direction of the resource and/or light we define we need.

Oftentimes if a plant is stuck or is languishing and withering, we do not blame the plant, we change the environment and/or resources it needs to survive, thrive, and then flourish.

Sometimes the plant needs to be transplanted and repotted; sometimes it just needs the proper resources it lacks allocated to it.

So whatever is missing, you need to name it to tame it. Once you name what needs to change, you need to consider whether you let the plant wither and languish or you change the resources allocated to the plant for it to heal and grow towards flourishing.

Therapist's Note:
Love

Your lover/partner should treat you better than the best qualities of those who love you the most, otherwise you are better off dating your best friend.

If your best friend treats you like shit, then maybe you need a new metric for what a friend is.

AND you will only Receive
and
Accept the Love you Believe you Deserve.

Storytime:
RelationShit

Therapist: So how have the discussions with your partner been going?

Client crying: They aren't. They said I need therapy and they want me fixed. They said they won't do therapy because they don't need it.

Therapist: Well, the homework was to see if they'd be open to couple's therapy to work on the relationship as a unit, not on individuals in it.

Client: Yeah… they said they don't want to do couple's therapy because I am the problem and they don't have time for therapy.

Therapist: What exactly did they say they wanted you to change?

Client: …

Therapist: I see. They just want you to change and be what they want, without telling you what that is.

Client: I used to just go with the flow because I wanted them happy. But I realized it was always about them and they are upset because now I am doing what I want to make me happy.

Therapist: What makes you happy?

Client: Being with friends and seeing my family. Since I have been with my partner, there is no time to see friends or family.

My parents are getting old. I just want to spend time with them.

Therapist: So your partner doesn't support you spending time with people you care about.

Has your partner ever wanted something and you supported them through it even if it meant you wouldn't get what you wanted?

Client: Yes. The entire relationship.

Therapist: So now you just are asking for the same support?

Client: Yes!

Therapist: Then why are you with your partner when they won't reciprocate back?

Client: I don't know anymore!!!

Therapist: Well one thing I do know is that whatever is going on, isn't working for you anymore. You have to decide if you want to change it or stay in it.

Guiding Principle # 3:

Learn to Embrace the Love that the people who love You the most Believe You Deserve.

Therapist's Reflection:

Sometimes the people that seem the hardest to love are the Ones that Need it the Most.

So if you really have a hard time loving yourself, know you deserve to be loved the most by yourself; just don't be an ass and go around demanding it like you are entitled to other people's love - start loving yourself and maybe others can start to Tolerate and even Accept You.

Also, please note, that the others who are hardest to love, who may need love the most, are not entitled to your Unconditional Love;

You aren't obligated to be the one to Love them the Most - That is their task to do, just as your own self acceptance and Self-Love is Your Task to do.

Guiding Principle # 4:

Always make Time for what is Important to You/ Waste no Time.

Therapist's Reflection:

Time is the only commodity that no amount of money can recreate or buy back. The only time we waste is the spent time we regret or resent.

Make room for what matters to you, and know you deserve love. (Everyone else is not as invested in you to begin with, so why do they get a say?)

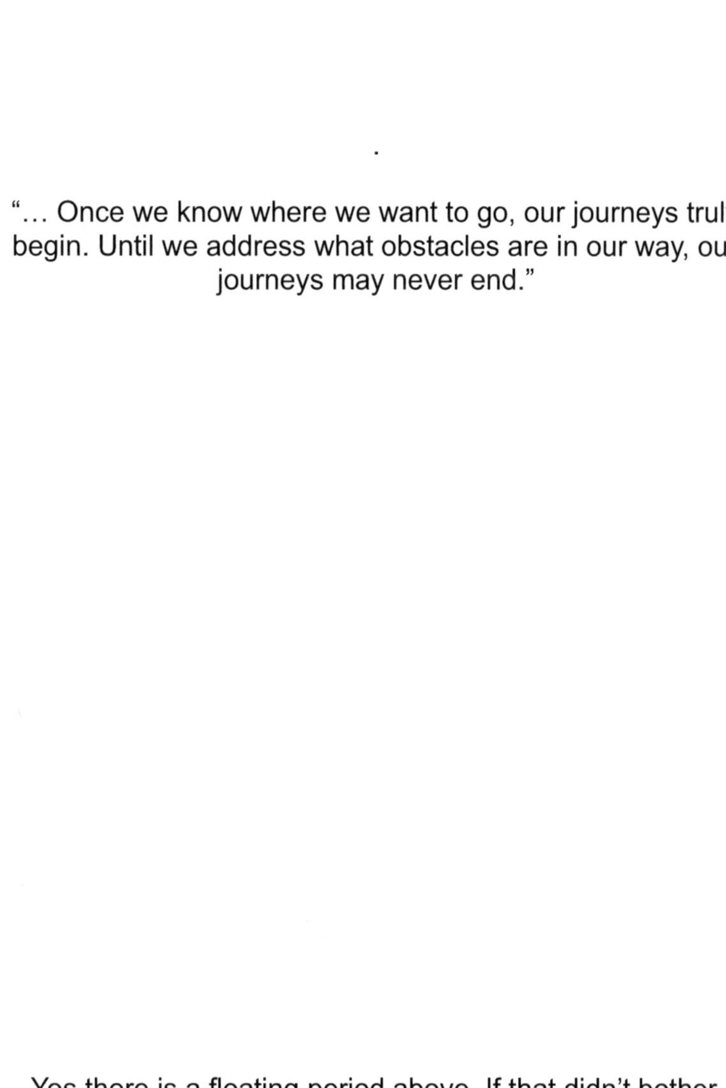

.

"… Once we know where we want to go, our journeys truly begin. Until we address what obstacles are in our way, our journeys may never end."

Yes there is a floating period above. If that didn't bother you or you didn't notice it- slow down.

Preparation for change…

Therapist's Note:
Change without Effort?

Yes, change "sometimes" requires you to do homework. It is self motivated, and self paced, and self reflective. So here is a conversation about doing homework... or self work...

Storytime:
Laziness

Client: I'm not good with homework…so I probably won't do anything you give me.

Therapist: I can tell…

Client:.. Yeah…

Therapist: If you actually gave a shit and prioritized it like the movies you watch, or music you listen to, or even dopamine foods and activities you do, we wouldn't be having this conversation. You probably wouldn't have to actually see me.

Client: I am here because I am lazy or unmotivated…

Therapy: I don't believe in "lazy" or unmotivated.

I believe in you, otherwise I'd refer you out.

I also believe that when people don't do something that benefits them, there is an unnamed reason even if they THINK they know what the reason is. Name it to tame it - what is your reason for not prioritizing yourself and exercising self determination?

Therapist's Lesson: Obstacles to Change

Three most common reasons why you might not do what benefits you:

1) You lack the energy

2) You lack the direction/instruction

3) You have competing priorities that may seem more urgent or appealing

Therapist's Lesson:
The Four Quests

Ask yourself these four questions to evaluate and name your situation/circumstance/choice/decision:

(Open ended questions for a thorough evaluation)

1) What purpose does it serve or what does it achieve?

2) What meaning does it have or why is it important to me?

3) The way it is, how does it satisfy my needs or contribute to my satisfaction?

4) The way it is, what am I actually committing to [doing]?

(Closed ended questions for a quick assessment)

1) Does it have a purpose or achieve something?

2) Does it have meaning or is it important to me?

3) The way it is, does it satisfy a need or make me happy?

4) The way it is, do I want to do it or continue with it?

Therapist's Lesson:
The Four Quests Parameters

If you are saying 'Yes' to four of the closed ended questions, it may be worthwhile to consider keeping your situation or sticking with your decision.

If you are saying 'Yes' to three of the closed ended questions, you can tolerate the situation or choice.

If you are saying 'Yes' to less than 3 of the closed ended questions, you can probably find a better replacement or better alternative than whatever situation you are in or choice you are making- in other words, you may be unsatisfied with how you are choosing to spend your energy and time, also known as wasting your fucking time!

If you say 'No' to questions three or four, ask yourself what needs to change for you to be satisfied/happy or for you to want to commit to the situation or choice.

Please remember: You have to name it to tame it.
Asking yourself the open ended questions helps you name specifics.

Once you name it, you can: Accept it, Change it, or Change your Expectation of what is named.

Storytime:
Smoke vs Fire

Client: I have anxiety/depression and get anxiety attacks/so depressed I can't get anything done.

Therapist: What contributes to your anxiety?

Client: Everything...

Therapist: When we see smoke, we know there is usually a fire somewhere. The smoke is the first thing we often see that indicates the fire. The smoke is often what incapacitates you; it cripples your senses and ability to respond effectively.

It is sometimes necessary to first address the smoke, but the goal is to find what is feeding the fire and cut it off so we can put the fire out.

Don't come to me wanting to only fan the smoke; we are here to address the fire and cut off what feeds it.

Sometimes fanning the smoke will only make the fire bigger. Other times it is necessary to diminish the smoke in order to get to the fire.

Just as I would leave that decision of fighting smoke vs fire vs both up to the fire experts, fire marshalls, and firefighters, allow me to step into my expertise and support you in addressing the relational and emotional smoke at appropriate times as we try to put out your trauma-inducing fires.

Client: How do I know what the fire or smoke is? What if I am just anxious?

Therapist: Anxiety and depression go hand in hand and in many cases overlap.

Sometimes anxiety causes depression. People get so anxious about failure, messing up, or rejection that they start to get crippled by that fear, they do nothing, and then they experience depression and poor self regard for feeling crippled..

Sometimes depression causes anxiety. People doubt themselves, lack energy, or feel so unmotivated they feel crippled by depression and then they get anxious about not getting anything done or failing the people around them.

Other times, the symptoms or smoke is caused by a third factor; usually chronic illness, ADHD/Autism/AuDHD/neurodiversity, or trauma. Let's see where the fire starts.

Therapist's Lesson:
What vs Why

Healing and change will take time. Set realistic expectations that it will take time. You will be undoing habits you engage in (often negative ones whether behaviors or thoughts you automatically have).

There is "What" you do and then there is "Why" you do it, which influences "How" you do it, and "How" it is experienced.

Healing and change will take time and repetition in order to replace the habitual thoughts, feelings, and actions we experience and have. Understanding the "Why" helps us understand the reason behind our habits and 'What' can change and "How" we can replace it.

The "What" is like smoke and the "Why" is the fire.

Prepare yourself to fight both smoke and fire.

Guiding Principle # 5:

We Grow, Achieve, and Succeed not when we are ready…
but When We are Willing.

Therapist's Reflection:

You may be tired of suffering and probably don't know life outside of misery; or maybe you don't know how to stop the suffering so you prioritize ways to numb yourself with distractions rather than dealing with the issue. Here is how you prepare for change.

First step: Be open, honest, and aware that something is in the way, it could be that you lack energy, lack direction, or have to handle something else more urgent.

Second step: Be compassionate to yourself the same way you would be compassionate with someone you love who is struggling.

Third step: **Make clear deliberate choices and commitments** to change things up.

Fourth step: Be willing to ask for help. Self-help for someone who feels helpless and has only known failure is kind of ironic and oxy-moronic.

A possibly necessary reminder: This book is NOT a self-help book - it is just a book of conversations that may be sardonically helpful...If you are seeking insight, this is when I redirect you to a professional.

Go seek a professional for non-self help.

“Sometimes it is not what you look for, but how we look at things that changes what we can see.”

Commitment to Change to Commencement of Change

Therapist's Note:
Principles

I won't tell you what to do or how to do it; you should consider adopting and committing to principles to create a containment for peace and healing space for yourself.

Identify what principles align with you, take the best of them and leave the rest of them.

Remember, if you are an Asshole to Anyone including Yourself - Hurt people will hurt people; people who are healing will heal people.

So start healing yourself or stay the fuck away from other people.

Storytime:
"Family"

Therapist: How was your weekend with your "family" this time?

Client: I'm so glad it's over. I can breathe again.

Therapist: If you dread them, why do you spend time with them?

Client: Because it is my family and I know them.

Therapist: People know misery well, doesn't mean it's good company. Do you want to have a positive relationship with them?

Client: That's impossible. I can't trust them.

Therapist: Can't or won't? If you can't, why can't you; and if you won't, why won't you?

Client: They can't be trusted because they lie and really care about themselves first.

Therapist: They are prioritizing their own healing. They can love you, and love themselves more.

If you cannot or will not trust them, they are not family; at best, they are roommates in a place you don't call home.

Therapist's Reflection: On Principles for Healing Vs Being Bound by Rules

It would be prudent to be guided by principles and not bound by rules for your healing journey and commitment to change.

Often, there are unspoken rules governing our relationships and within our families.Those unbending rules may lead to conflict between what we value and what we choose to do.

Being bound by rules sets you up for failure because you either follow them or break them.

Identifying principles to live by allows us room to grow and redirect. Being guided by principles allows you the flexibility to explore when things do not align as a straight path, to which you can adjust the course of your path or adjust the principles.

What are your principles for identifying family?

Guiding Principle # 6

Commit to Being Guided by Principles -
Not Bound by Rules.

Commit to living while being guided by principles
Not living by/ for appearances of being principled.

Guiding Principle # 7

Family is Whom you Choose, not whom you are related to;
those are relatives.
(We don't always Trust our relatives).

Choose your family wisely. Family is when you know You Matter, AND you know You Belong, AND You are Safe.

Therapist's Note:
What if I can't trust myself to change?

Then trust a trained professional to guide you to defining what trustworthy is and how you can become trustworthy to yourself.

Remember, because you can't trust yourself you will doubt your progress even if you made a change.

When you doubt yourself, you won't be able to fully commit to change or even effectively give voice to your needs.

If you remain silent and do not name what you don't trust about yourself, you cannot change your trustworthiness to yourself.

Your self doubt and poor self regard/image can act like an Inner Demon. Don't let it run wild in your mind - otherwise that place becomes a dangerous space to dwell alone.

Storytime:
Suffering in Silence

Client: I just...

Therapist waits a few minutes in silence

Therapist: Sometimes we fear sounding silly, stupid, or judged for our accents or our lack of academic vernacular; Sometimes we have difficulty completing our thoughts or sentences.

It's okay. Say it ugly and broken. If you say it, it gives me the chance to clarify and seek to understand you. But if you say nothing at all, I will never get to know you or the damned demons in your head and heart and our sessions would be overpriced lying sessions.

When your inner demons are left unaddressed, they can grow to haunt everyone else around you - even if your anxiety tries to prevent that stress on others through avoidance.

It is safe to practice finding your confidence and voice here. Practice with me so you don't practice on your loved ones or coworkers.

Client: ... umm okay, I'll try.

Therapist: Or you can also just tell me to fuck off and fire me - your problem, not mine.

Therapist's Lesson:
Adopted from the Poem:
"In Silence" originally written by yours untruly, me.
"Speak the Truth Ugly"

In silence,
You waited.
Then realize
Your silence
Is unheard,
And because
of silence,
You still wait.

So speak up-
Speak ugly.
Do not fear
How you sound.

Speak open
Speak silly
Speak aloud
With accents
With a twang
With no care

Focus on
Being heard-
And to be
Understood
And with an
Open mind

So commit
To be heard,
To be known,
To be seen
Say it out-
Speak Ugly

Guiding Principle # 8

Be Okay with Saying it Ugly.
(Then we can call it the Ugly Truth).

Guiding Principle # 9

Stop feeding Your Inner Demons, otherwise they May grow to Haunt the People around You.

Fight/Silence your Inner Demons so they will not Haunt the People around You.

Therapist's Reflection:

Once you can name them and say it ugly and speak their truth aloud, then you can effectively work to challenge and change the nature of those demons.

What Inner Demons are holding you back? Do you have a name for those demons?

"I actually didn't know if it would work. Funny thing is, half the time I am not sure anything I try will work..."

Maintaining Momentum

Therapist's Note:

The following guiding principles are for you to explore and possibly adopt.

Because I have no energy to continue to expand on stories, lessons, or reflections, I will let you do that on your own or with somebody else.

If you have issues understanding these principles or find that the principles feel offensive, get therapy - you sound like a real pain in the ass for other people around you.

Again, a not-so-gentle reminder: This isn't a self- help book - we already determined if you are seeking a ~~self-~~help book because you are in need of help, you may not be able to help yourself without guidance.

Guiding Principle # (Insert arbitrary number)

Ask more Questions rather than trying to Answer them.

Therapist's Reflections:

When you ask more questions, you find more answers about yourself even if you never answer the actual question.

If you are confused by this, try asking a different question.

Guiding Principle # (Insert arbitrary number)

Allow the Hurt to Define the Healing.

Therapist's Reflections:

If you hurt someone, you do not get to define their healing - they get to decide if you are trustworthy.

If someone hurts you, they do not get to define your healing - you get to decide if they are trustworthy.

If you hurt yourself... well just don't do it because that gets complicated. How do you decide when/if you are trustworthy to yourself? Get a fucking therapist!

Guiding Principle # (Insert arbitrary number)

Do what You Love, or Learn to Love what You Do.

Therapist's Reflection:

Moving in the direction of love is important. Otherwise you are wasting your time; however, if what you do is leading to something you love, then that is all planned and not a waste of time at all.

Remember, the only time wasted is time we regret, resent, or don't learn anything from.

Guiding Principle # (Insert arbitrary number)

Do away with “Good”, “Bad”, “Right” or “Wrong”. Adopt “Healthy” vs “UnHealthy” and “Helpful” vs “UnHelpful”

Therapist’s Reflection:

What is “good” to a starving thief is “bad” to the unwitting donor.

If you are fixated by “good” vs “bad” and “right” vs “wrong” then you may be part of the asshole group that benefits from and is privileged by those rules or you don’t want the accountability of making decisions regarding complex situations in which humanity conflicts with human interpreted rules (that benefit you).

Guiding Principle # (Insert arbitrary number)

Be Accountable for the Impact of your Intentions and Actions.

Therapist's Reflections:

Oftentimes we try to justify or excuse our impact by defending our intentions. Intentions are ideas that we assume are warranted, wanted, or needed.

Leave nothing to "guessing" and don't make assumptions. Don't go being proud of making the best hammer for someone when they may have wanted/needed a screwdriver.

So fuck your intentions and understand and own how your ideas, when implemented, may impact others and yourself.

“There is no going out of my way for you, when you are the Destination.”

Final Thoughts

Congratulations!

If you made it this far without losing your shit, you *MIGHT* not be a narcissist.

I hope this book encouraged you to get therapy; helped make therapy a little easier; or helped you so much that you don't ~~believe you~~ need a therapist.

However, after reading this book, if you think you are a victim of everyone around you, or if you had difficulty owning how you contribute to a situation without defending yourself, you may actually be a narcissist. If that's the case, this book wasn't for you - this book was for the other people that have to deal with you.

Pssst.. Wait.. there's more!! In case you thought your shit was healed… think again!

“We are cursed by our own faults (flaws).”

Familiar Habits

Therapist's Note:
Old Habits Die Hard

When we are tired, hungry, or stressed, we revert back to what is familiar, our oldest or most ingrained habits - at least until we deeply embed new habits.

Storytime:
Failure

Client: I know you gave me homework and shit to do. I didn't do it.

Therapist: You cursed. Either you are frustrated or you learned how to curse from me. So you are learning something in therapy.

Client chuckles: I am tired of failing. I plan to change things, I try it out, and then I forget and fail to change. I end up doing the same shit or reacting the same way I have always done before.

Therapist: That's part of change. Failing and learning from it. You may never succeed, but if you learn, you won't quite lose or fail either. You are refining what works.

Client: I guess. But how long will it take?

Therapist: As long as it needs to in order for you to break automatic habits. So it will require very deliberate change and action. If you are tired, hungry, or stressed then you will revert back to what is habitual.

Our brains like efficiency, so it will always go back to what feels automatic or easy. So practice the new habit until it becomes second nature and therefore efficient. When you are rested, practice the habit more. If you only try to enact the change when things are stressful or when you are frustrated, you will build unhelpful form. Like any athlete, you do drills when you are rested to build a more optimal form for responding to things.

Client: But I am tired all the time! I either don't get enough sleep or I forget to eat.

Therapist: Well shit, then the first habits to change are your sleep and eating schedules. **Start (t)here**.

Therapist's Lesson: Working your Way Back

To even break a habit, you will have to be aware of it. Once you are aware of the habit, you can start to change it. So as you begin to name these obstacles, you will be able to start addressing them.

Remember that change will take time and you are in the process of naming the things that do not work, as well as becoming aware of unhealthy or unhelpful habits you were not even aware you had.

If you think changing the way you brush your teeth is hard (and you do that maybe at most 5 times a day), then imagine how difficult it is to change the habits that you experience 100 times an hour such as doubt, anxiety, and defeat.

The process will feel like you are going backwards, however, you are going upstream and starting from the source. You are getting to what feeds the fire that plumes your smoke.

Throughout the process, be patient, be kind, and stay deliberate - because you WILL revert back to old habits when you are hungry, tired, or stressed. AND you will slowly but surely, build healthier and more helpful habits with deliberate practice and effort.

Guiding Principle # (Who the fuck is keeping track anyway?)

Work on whatever is in the Way of the Work.

Therapist's Final Reflection:

Whatever is in the way of the work you are wanting to do, is really the work you have to do, to get your way to actually work.

Our habits, our doubts, and our distractions are the obstacles to our work and are therefore our work.

Name the habits, distractions, and doubts.

If you didn't cause it, don't dwell too much on it - it isn't yours to heal or hold.

If you can't change it, then change your expectation of it or accept it and move on.

If you can't control it, refocus your energy to what you can control.

It is also okay to stop trying to help yourself and seek help instead.

If you feel stuck, go seek professional help. You are in the way of your own work and a professional may be needed to help you get past yourself.

“Hell is repeating something over and over again, and hating it.”

Repetition, Repetition, Repetition

Therapist's Note:
These pages are to fulfill a certain distributor's 76 page minimum.

This section was created to meet the minimum requirements in order to print the hardcover version of my book.

Statements in this section are written so there may not be any disparaging damages.

An alleged particular distributor, who shall not be named and but shall remain questionable, may or may not be trustworthy.

If I do not print a hardcover of my book, a particular printer and distributor may or may not duplicate my work and print a hardcover version as they may or may not retain rights to do so under the distributor's agreement. If the particular printer and distributor engage in such acts and render the product for sale, I receive no royalties from the hardback version they sell of my work. This may or may not have already been done with one of my other works.

So this page will be repeated to fill in the minimum requirements and maintain control of my works.

Therapist's Note:
These pages are to fulfill a certain distributor's 76 page minimum.

This section was created to meet the minimum requirements in order to print the hardcover version of my book.

Statements in this section are written so there may not be any disparaging damages.

An alleged particular distributor, who shall not be named and but shall remain questionable, may or may not be trustworthy.

If I do not print a hardcover of my book, a particular printer and distributor may or may not duplicate my work and print a hardcover version as they may or may not retain rights to do so under the distributor's agreement. If the particular printer and distributor engage in such acts and render the product for sale, I receive no royalties from the hardback version they sell of my work. This may or may not have already been done with one of my other works.

So this page will be repeated to fill in the minimum requirements and maintain control of my works.

Therapist's Note:
These pages are to fulfill a certain distributor's 76 page minimum.

This section was created to meet the minimum requirements in order to print the hardcover version of my book.

Statements in this section are written so there may not be any disparaging damages.

An alleged particular distributor, who shall not be named and but shall remain questionable, may or may not be trustworthy.

If I do not print a hardcover of my book, a particular printer and distributor may or may not duplicate my work and print a hardcover version as they may or may not retain rights to do so under the distributor's agreement. If the particular printer and distributor engage in such acts and render the product for sale, I receive no royalties from the hardback version they sell of my work. This may or may not have already been done with one of my other works.

So this page will be repeated to fill in the minimum requirements and maintain control of my works.

Therapist's Note:
These pages are to fulfill a certain distributor's 76 page minimum.

This section was created to meet the minimum requirements in order to print the hardcover version of my book.

Statements in this section are written so there may not be any disparaging damages.

An alleged particular distributor, who shall not be named and but shall remain questionable, may or may not be trustworthy.

If I do not print a hardcover of my book, a particular printer and distributor may or may not duplicate my work and print a hardcover version as they may or may not retain rights to do so under the distributor's agreement. If the particular printer and distributor engage in such acts and render the product for sale, I receive no royalties from the hardback version they sell of my work. This may or may not have already been done with one of my other works.

So this page will be repeated to fill in the minimum requirements and maintain control of my works.

Thank you for reading this far and for supporting authors, artists, and creators of various forms.

Made in the USA
Columbia, SC
13 July 2024

0e5ba3f4-a9f3-4a90-8a86-93ba5b7a5f67R01